CREATING
HORROR
COMICS

DAVID BELMONTE

NEW YORK

Published in 2015 by The Rosen Publishing Group, Inc.
29 East 21st Street, New York, NY 10010

First Edition

Text: Lisa Regan and Joe Harris
Illustrations: David Belmonte (Beehive Illustration)
Design: Notion Design
Editor: Joe Harris

Library of Congress Cataloging-in-Publication Data

Belmonte, David.
Creating horror comics / by David Belmonte.
p. cm. -- (Creating comics)
Includes index.
ISBN 978-1-4777-5920-2 (library binding)
1. Horror comic books, strips, etc. -- Technique -- Juvenile literature. 2. Monsters in art -- Juvenile literature. 3. Cartooning -- Technique -- Juvenile literature. I. Belmonte, David. II. Title.
NC1764.8.M65 B45 2015
741.5--d23

Printed in the United States

SL004331US

CPSIA Compliance Information: Batch #CW15PK: For further information contact Rosen Publishing, New York, New York at 1-800-237-9932

CONTENTS

TOOLS OF THE TRADE

YOU DON'T NEED EXPENSIVE EQUIPMENT TO START MAKING HORROR COMICS. THE MOST IMPORTANT TOOL IS YOUR OWN IMAGINATION!

PENCILS

Soft (B, 2B) pencils are great for drawing loosely and are easy to erase. Fine point pencils are handy for adding detail.

ERASERS

A kneaded eraser molds to shape, so you can use it to remove pencil from tiny areas. Keep a clean, square-edged eraser to hand, too.

PENS

An artist's pens are his or her most precious tools! Gather a selection with different tips for varying the thickness of your line work.

FINE LINE AND BRUSH PENS

Fine line pens are excellent for small areas of detail. Brush pens are perfect for varying your line weight or shading large areas.

PENCILS, INKS, AND COLORS

THERE ARE FOUR STAGES IN THE DRAWING PROCESS. IF YOU FOLLOW THIS METHOD, IT WILL SAVE YOU FROM SPOTTING BASIC MISTAKES WHEN IT IS TOO LATE TO FIX THEM!

ROUGH SKETCHES

Start by roughly sketching your character. Work out their pose and proportions before adding any details.

TIGHT SKETCHES

When you are happy with the basic frame, you can tighten it up with firm pencil strokes, then add in some detail.

INKS

Ink over your best pencil lines. Vary the thickness of your strokes, and add dramatic shadows. Then erase your pencil lines.

COLORS

You can leave your drawings in black and white or add color. Your palette for horror stories will be quite dark.

DRAWING HUMAN FIGURES

SOME OF THE MONSTERS IN YOUR HORROR STORIES MAY HAVE WEIRD PROPORTIONS. HOWEVER, YOU WILL NEED TO BE ABLE TO DRAW SOME REALISTIC HUMANS TO ACT AS YOUR HEROES. GET THE BASICS RIGHT, AND THEN YOU CAN ADD DETAIL.

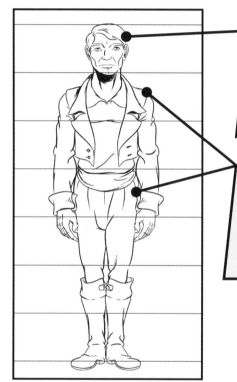

HEADS
Think of your characters' height in terms of a number of "heads." A typical human character is about seven heads tall.

SHOULDERS AND HIPS
Male characters are broadest at their shoulders. Female characters have hips and shoulders wider than their waists.

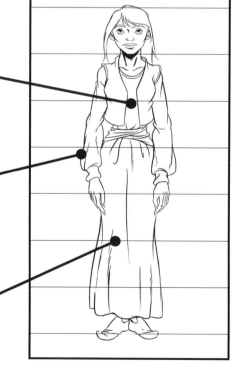

TORSOS
This female is shorter than the male, so to remain in proportion, her body is slightly shorter.

ARMS
Arms reach from the shoulder down to the midthigh. Make sure they aren't too long, though, or your characters will look like apes!

LEGS
Most characters' legs measure about four head lengths from hips to toes.

DRAWING HEADS

THE BEST WAY TO PRACTICE DRAWING FACES IS TO LOOK AT REAL PEOPLE. THE MIRROR CAN BE A VERY HELPFUL TOOL! YOU WILL ALSO WANT TO BEAR IN MIND THESE BASIC RULES.

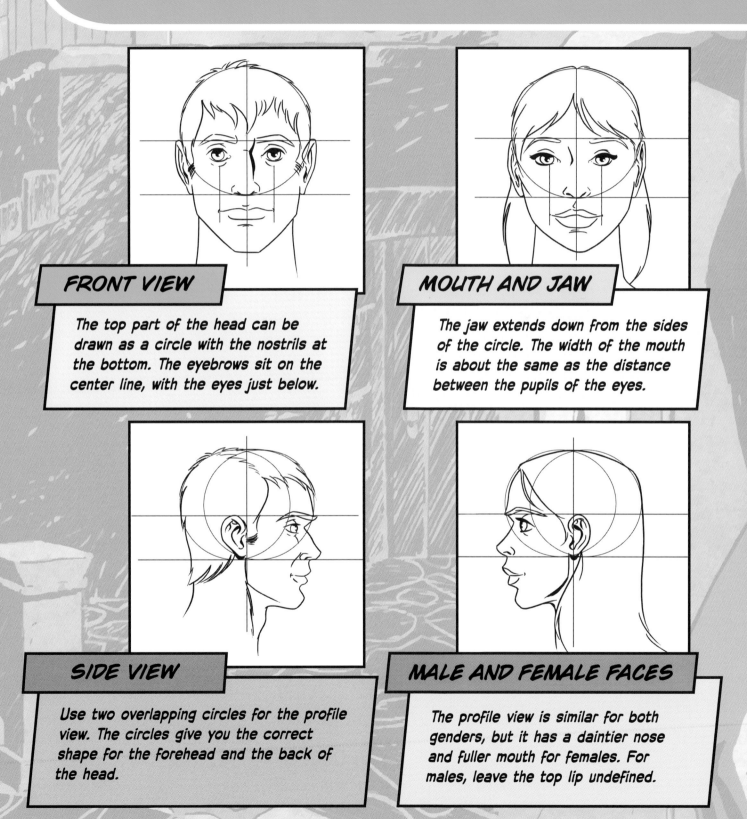

FRONT VIEW

The top part of the head can be drawn as a circle with the nostrils at the bottom. The eyebrows sit on the center line, with the eyes just below.

MOUTH AND JAW

The jaw extends down from the sides of the circle. The width of the mouth is about the same as the distance between the pupils of the eyes.

SIDE VIEW

Use two overlapping circles for the profile view. The circles give you the correct shape for the forehead and the back of the head.

MALE AND FEMALE FACES

The profile view is similar for both genders, but it has a daintier nose and fuller mouth for females. For males, leave the top lip undefined.

A SWAMP ZOMBIE

THIS CREEPY CREATURE HAS BEEN LYING IN WAIT BENEATH THE FOUL, STAGNANT WATERS OF AN ANCIENT SWAMP. NOW IT HAS FINALLY EMERGED, AND IT LOOKS LIKES IT'S HUNGRY FOR HUMAN FLESH! CAN YOU CAPTURE ITS FRIGHTENING POSE AND EXPRESSION?

1 Use a wireframe to plan how you want your creature to stand and how long its limbs will be. It's tall and skinny.

2 Develop the hands and feet, with fingers and toes. Use curved lines to outline the thin legs and arms. Connect the hips and chest with a narrow waist, and sketch in facial features.

3 Add more details. Work up the hollow face with its gaping mouth. Add holes for the eyes and nose. Begin to sketch the loose rags hanging from its body. Use scratchy lines to create ragged edges.

4 Erase any guide lines you no longer need, and finish off the details of the creature's clothes, face, and hair. Its ribs are clearly visible underneath its cold, damp flesh. Add small details, such as buttons on its shirt and holes in its pants.

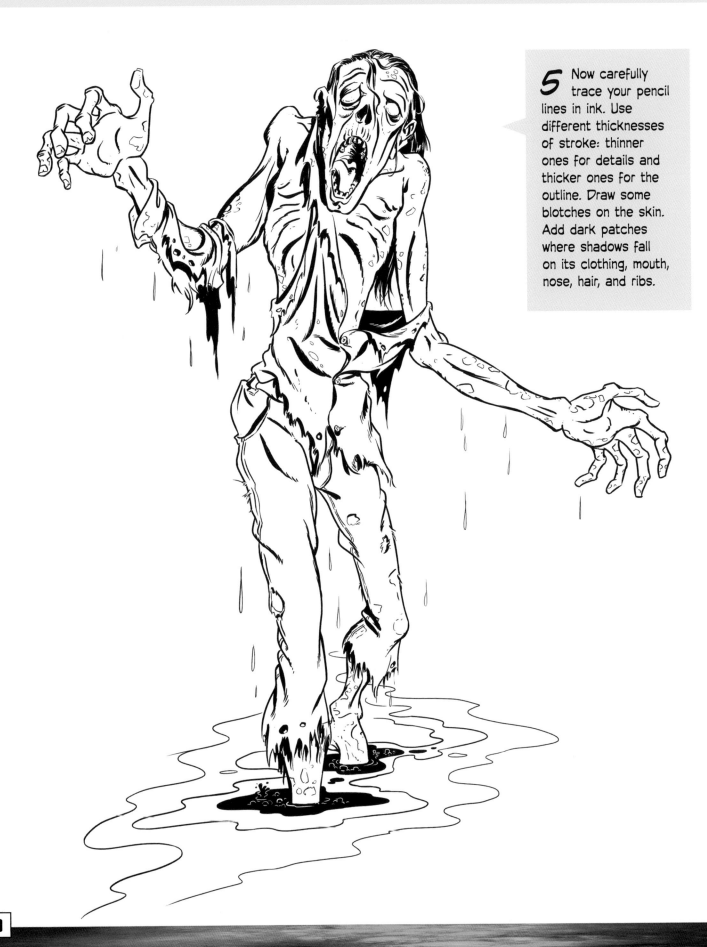

5 Now carefully trace your pencil lines in ink. Use different thicknesses of stroke: thinner ones for details and thicker ones for the outline. Draw some blotches on the skin. Add dark patches where shadows fall on its clothing, mouth, nose, hair, and ribs.

6 You can use color to suggest texture and temperature in a picture like this. The green and blue colors we have chosen make this swamp zombie look deathly cold. The yellow sheen on its flesh and clothes make it look slimy and damp.

SHADOWS AND ATMOSPHERE

A SCENE CAN BE COMPLETELY TRANSFORMED BY THE EFFECTIVE USE OF SHADOWS. A SETTING THAT WOULD APPEAR ORDINARY OR EVEN WELCOMING IN GOOD LIGHTING CAN SUDDENLY BECOME MYSTERIOUS AND SINISTER.

A SCENE WITHOUT SHADOWS

This library scene could be any ordinary library, although the costumes give a visual clue that it is a historical setting. The light source is unclear: Is light streaming through the stained-glass window or coming from the ceiling lamp?

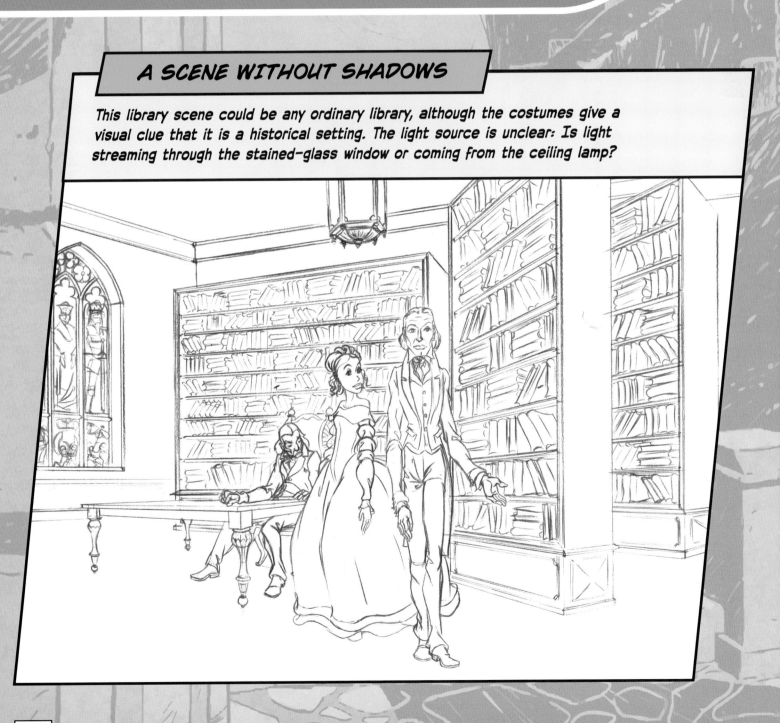

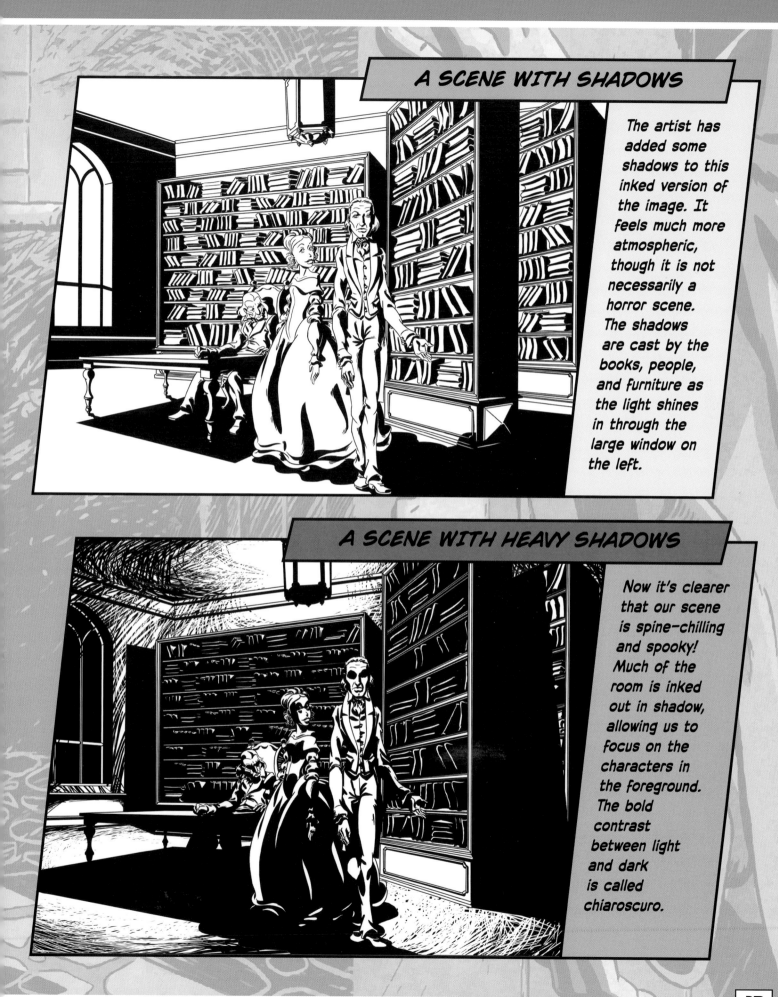

A SCENE WITH SHADOWS

The artist has added some shadows to this inked version of the image. It feels much more atmospheric, though it is not necessarily a horror scene. The shadows are cast by the books, people, and furniture as the light shines in through the large window on the left.

A SCENE WITH HEAVY SHADOWS

Now it's clearer that our scene is spine-chilling and spooky! Much of the room is inked out in shadow, allowing us to focus on the characters in the foreground. The bold contrast between light and dark is called chiaroscuro.

AN ANCIENT VAMPIRE

THE OLDER VAMPIRES GET, THE MORE POWERFUL THEY BECOME. THEY ALSO APPEAR LESS AND LESS HUMAN—SOME LOOK MORE LIKE BATS THAN PEOPLE. THIS BLOODSUCKER HAS BEEN ALIVE FOR MANY CENTURIES, AS YOU CAN TELL FROM HIS OLD-FASHIONED CLOTHES AND UGLY FACE.

1 Sketch a wireframe with ovals for his head, chest, and pelvis. Draw lines to place his limbs the way you want them.

2 Add the swirl of his coattails. Begin to put flesh on his bones (but not much) with long, lean legs and arms and a slender torso. Draw his hands and face in a little more detail.

3 Take time to sketch some old-fashioned clothes, such as a frilled shirt, tall boots, and a high collar. Add detail to his long, pointed ears and gaping, snakelike mouth. Notice how his knees and waist are exceptionally thin.

4 Now go over the whole figure again, adding in final details such as the pupils of his eyes. Erase any guide lines that you no longer need. Make sure that all your lines are clean, crisp, and accurate.

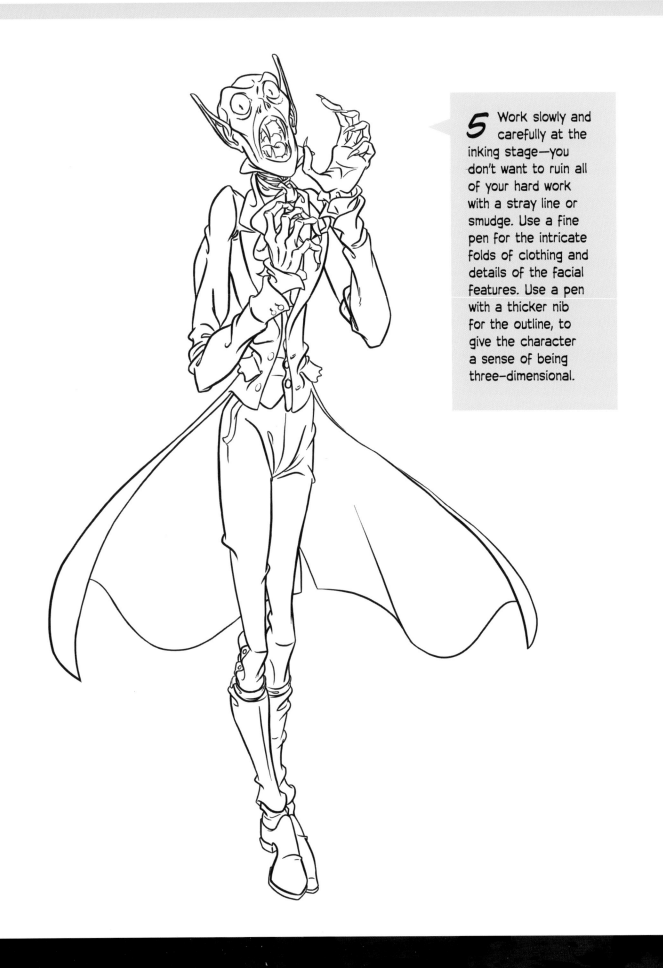

5 Work slowly and carefully at the inking stage—you don't want to ruin all of your hard work with a stray line or smudge. Use a fine pen for the intricate folds of clothing and details of the facial features. Use a pen with a thicker nib for the outline, to give the character a sense of being three-dimensional.

6 Don't put your inking pen down just yet! Our vampire's outfit is largely a wash of black ink, but we have used a brown highlight to show contours and folds. The evil creature is lit from below, which creates an eerie effect. The light shining on his bony hands and face is shown as yellow highlights, and his eyes glow with a sinister red light.

EXPRESSIONS AND BODY LANGUAGE

TO CREATE A SENSE OF ATMOSPHERE IN A HORROR COMIC, YOU WILL NEED TO BE ABLE TO MAKE YOUR CHARACTERS PERFORM LIKE ACTORS! BY SHOWING HOW THEY RESPOND TO A SITUATION, YOU CAN MAKE READERS CARE ABOUT WHAT IS HAPPENING.

RELAXED

This character is standing with her weight on her back foot, and her head is cocked slightly to one side. Her shoulders are relaxed and her hands hang loosely.

NERVOUS

This girl's wide eyes and clenched hands show she is worried about something. Her shoulders are raised and she leans forward, ready to run if necessary.

SCARED

This guy is terrified! He has thrown up one hand in self-defense, while his other feels for an escape route. His eyebrows have shot up into his hair. His eyes and mouth show his fear.

CONFIDENT

If this dude is scared, he's not showing it! Chest out, arms back, he's ready to take on any monsters. The determined look on his face says he's a hero. Or is he just overconfident?

A HAUNTED SCARECROW

THIS PUMPKIN-HEADED SCARECROW HAS BEEN BROUGHT TO LIFE BY A SPIRIT OF VENGEANCE FROM BEYOND THE GRAVE. BEWARE OF ITS CLAWLIKE HANDS AND SHARP-PRONGED PITCHFORK! WHAT KIND OF SPOOKY STORIES WILL IT INSPIRE YOU TO ILLUSTRATE?

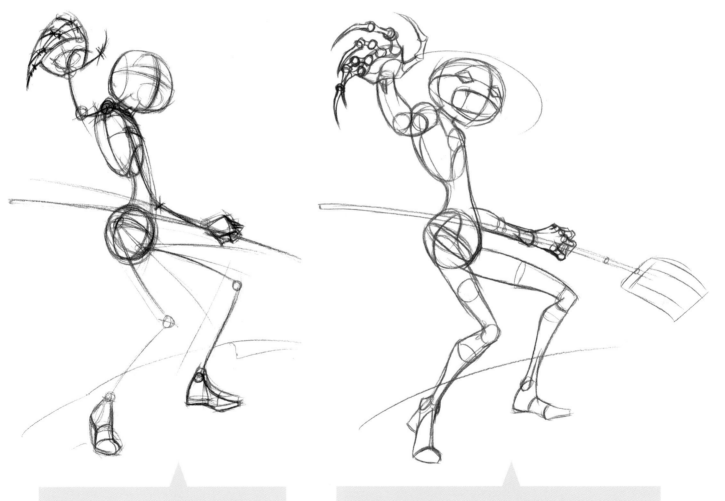

1 Body language plays an important role in making a creature look sinister. Is this scarecrow warning us away from something?

2 Bulk out its frame, giving definition to its skinny arms and legs. Take time to sketch each joint and knuckle for its outstretched, clawlike hand.

3 This picture uses foreshortening to show the creature reaching toward us. The leading hand is much larger than the trailing one, because it is closer to the viewer. Sketch the features on its gruesome face, and add detail to its clothing.

4 Add details, such as the texture of the hat and the folds, rips, and roughly stitched seams of the clothes. Make sure that you have all of the important details in place, then erase any unnecessary lines before moving on.

5 Ink your scarecrow carefully with a black pen. You will need to use very fine lines for the textural details, such as the straw poking through its clothing. Use a slightly broader pen for its outline. Then fill in the shadows on its shins and feet and the black grass.

6 We have added in more shadows at the coloring stage. Use dark blocks of color for the body and grabbing hand, with pale highlights on the left edge of each shape to give it definition. The pumpkin head is glowing from within, so the brightest orange appears in the mouth and eyes.

TELLING A HORROR STORY

THERE ARE MANY DIFFERENT WAYS TO TELL A COMIC STORY. AN ARTIST IS LIKE A FILM DIRECTOR AND MUST CHOOSE THE BEST ANGLES AND DISTANCES FOR EACH PANEL. IN THIS SHORT STORY, WE SHOW AN EXPLORER OPENING A MYSTERIOUS STONE DOOR, ONLY TO BE GREETED BY A WEREWOLF!

WEREWOLF ATTACK! FIRST ATTEMPT

This version of the scene isn't terrible, but it's a little static and boring. The panels are all the same size. The "actors" are shown from a similar distance, and the viewpoints chosen do not do enough to create a sense of urgency or drama. The reader understands the story but is not drawn in.

WEREWOLF ATTACK! SECOND ATTEMPT

This second version of the scene is much more exciting. The panel shapes are interesting, and close-up shots are mixed with longer shots and varied angles. However, there is so much going on that the scene has become confused. And what is happening in the last panel? Is it even in the same place?

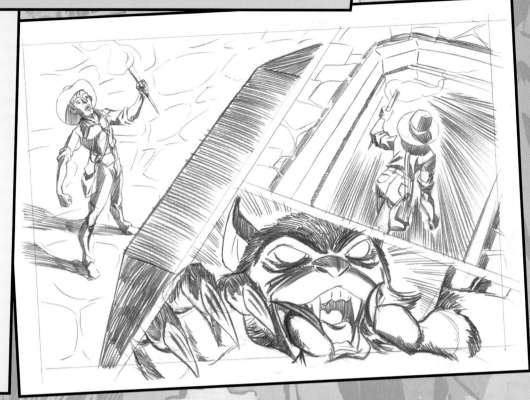

WEREWOLF ATTACK! THIRD ATTEMPT

This third version of the scene gets the balance just right. The storytelling is nice and clear—it's not hard for the reader to tell what has happened. However, there is plenty of variation in the distance and angle from which we see the action, and there is a well-planned sense of drama and excitement.

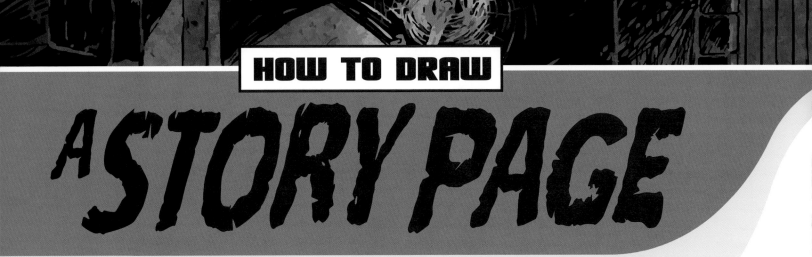

HOW TO DRAW A STORY PAGE

COMIC ART IS ABOUT MORE THAN JUST INDIVIDUAL IMAGES! A REAL COMIC ARTIST TELLS A DYNAMIC STORY THROUGH A SEQUENCE OF PANELS. IN THIS FINAL PROJECT, YOU CAN PUT TOGETHER ALL THE SKILLS YOU'VE LEARNED IN THIS BOOK TO CREATE A FINISHED COMICS PAGE.

1 Decide what your story is and how many frames you need to tell it. Then create a rough sketch of the page. Don't try to fit too much into each frame. In our first panel, the scene is set with a character at the foot of a creepy staircase. In the second and third panels, they approach a door and open it to reveal what's inside. Then the main action happens in the final panel, when the character is revealed as a monster!

2 Take a careful look at your rough page. Do you want to make any changes before you add details to the pencil sketches? We decided to flip the first panel around, so that the reader's eye falls on the shadow on the staircase before anything else. This creates a nice sense of tension. Notice the way that the jumping character in the final panel overlaps with the top edge of the panel. It's an excellent way of giving a panel extra excitement.

3 We've really gone to town with the shadows in the inking stage. By using plenty of black, you can show readers that this is a chilling tale and put them on edge. Notice that we have not lost any detail, though, because we have used narrow white lines to show shapes and textures within the shadowy areas.

4 The color version of this story cleverly uses light and shade, too. Your eye seeks the detail in the top scene, and then it is drawn to the light farther down. Clever details, such as the yellow keyhole in frame two, link the panels together and give visual clues to what is happening and where the action is taking place.

CHIAROSCURO
(kee-yahr-oh-SKYOO-ro)
An art technique that uses lots of contrast between light and dark.

EMBELLISH (em-BEHL-lish)
To add extra details.

EXTEND (eks-TEND)
To make longer.

FORESHORTENING
(fohr-SHORE-teh-ning)
Changing real proportions to show that an object is close or far away.

INTRICATE (IN-trih-kit)
Featuring lots of detail.

PALETTE (PAL-lit)
The selection of colors used in an image or story.

PERSPECTIVE (per-SPEK-tiv)
Showing three dimensions on a two-dimensional drawing, with smaller items in the distance.

PROFILE (PROH-file)
A view from the side.

PROPORTIONS
(pruh-POHR-shuhnz)
The size of an object, such as a body part, in relation to other elements of an image.

SINISTER (SIH-nis-tuhr)
Threatening of evil or harm.

STAGNANT (STAG-nent)
(of water) Not flowing, and therefore probably poisonous and bad-smelling.

WIREFRAME (WYRE-fraym)
The basic outline sketch of a character, showing posture and proportion.

FURTHER INFORMATION

FURTHER READING

Jantner, Janos. *Drawing Horror Movie Monsters.* New York: PowerKids Press, 2013.

Tallarico, Tony. *Drawing and Cartooning Monsters: A Step-by-Step Guide for the Aspiring Monster-Maker.* Mineola, NY: Dover, 2010.

Zalme, Ron. *How to Draw Goosebumps.* New York: Scholastic, 2010.

WEBSITES

Due to the changing nature of internet links, PowerKids Press has developed an online list of sites related to the subject of this book. This site is updated regularly. Please use this link to access the list:

www.powerkidslinks.com/cc/horror

INDEX